C000135006

Enchanted Things

signposts to a new nomadism

Phil Smith

To Richard
best wishes,

Triarchy Press

Phil Smith

ISBN: 978-1-909470-35-4

Published by Triarchy Press
www.triarchypress.net

The right of Phil Smith to be identified
as the author of th1s work has been
asserted by him in accordance with the
Copyright, Design and Patents Act 1988.

I stop for a moment. I look about me. Something slightly 'off' catches my eye: an incomplete sign that teeters toward the absurd, a rusted doorway that triggers a rare feeling of conviction, a tree shaped like a pinball machine, the remains of a windscreen glittering like emeralds, a fence just a little too bright for a barrier, a toy bigger than it ought to be. Such combinations of things and feelings have been the objects of my explorations and collections for some time now. In my experience, the more ordinary the place the more likely it is that discordance and its accompanying 'fanged noumena' will pop up; and the more deeply will the anxieties that falteringly accompany them burrow.

Such surprises were once the highlights
of my wandering in everyday urban and
rural spaces. But the times are changing
and these anomalies are massing in
such quantities today as to elbow the
ordinary aside, re-enchanting everyday
spaces and rendering 'the road' once
more open to nomadism. What I once
perceived as glancing and unexpected
encounters that cheered a moment on a
long walk, are increasingly manifest as
choruses of uncoordinated yelling from
the sides of the road like particularly
unruly spectators at a parade; and that is
changing what is possible, for those of us
who wander in the gaps in the everyday,
from short 'drifts' to something more like
a permanent *dérive*.

The enchanted and noisy objects and spaces are emerging under conditions of unprecedented mobility, and of imaginary and social liquefaction. The world is on the move; seas rise, villages are emptied, coastlines are redrawn, deserts spread to the suburbs, snowfall increases and lost battlefields and their barnacle-blistered artillery re-emerge. Only soap operas give any impression of permanence. Traditional fortresses like home, dwelling and nation are increasingly exposed as porous, fabricated and expensive things. The ways are opening, in a manner unprecedented for centuries, for a pervasive and benevolent nomadism, a new art of living, on both grand and individuated scales.

Such is the intensity of change, that it leaves neither distinctive city space nor natural terrain. The days when bounds could be beaten unselfconsciously are, of course, long gone, but now the nostalgic revival of such anachronisms signals the disappearance of the very boundaries themselves. The same files are shared between high-rise flat and rose-covered cottage. Culture and crime have never been so stylistically incoherent nor so geographically uniform. Commodities and images are feral.

Virtually unrestricted, commodification and distribution have removed the mental hedgerows between urban and rural 'fields'. Management and intervention – whether it be Enron running a floor trading in its own profits or Putin shooting stray dogs in Sochi – are far wilder and more authentically red in tooth and claw than any present-day wilderness. Countryside is almost entirely imaginary; so ephemeral it can be served up as entertainment before Olympic track and field.

To some extent, all this has always
been true, but never before with such
brazen intensity. Though you will be
disappointed if you expect to engage in
public discussion about such things.

These developments are combined and
uneven; unprecedented freedoms as likely
to be expressed in free-ranging digital
trajectories of finance as in human-
shaped luxuries. The emergence of a
new fundamentalism as likely to be the
last twitch of a choking authoritarianism
as the emergence of a reactionary
generation.

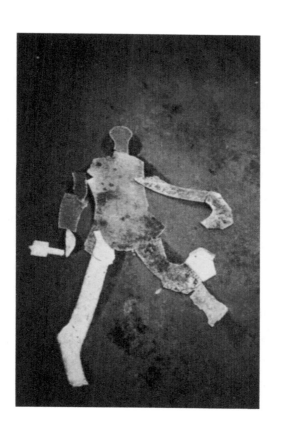

Increased rates of circulation of objects
and images and the disappearance of
bounds have conjured an unprecedentedly
predictable manifestation of the
unexpected in the everyday; not only
are there no jobs for life, but with the
acceleration of gender reassignment, the
growing army of cognitive behavioural
therapists, Mexican Waves, increases in
instances of normosis and the growing
influence of governmental behavioural
insights teams, increasingly there are
no lives for life. Deregulation has given
reregulation its day.

If, like me, you do not hold authenticity
in high regard, then you may consider
this replacement of distinct boundaries
and essential meanings with flimsy
fabrications as no bad thing. Indeed,
it may represent the beginnings of an
uneven re-enchantment of a landscape
long drained by reformation, enclosure,
utilitarianism, reformism and a narrowly
materialist enlightenment. Ironically, it is
those who hold disappearing authenticities
dearest, those who would hold my disdain
in the deepest contempt, who are the most
militant propagators of tales of a general
disenchantment; and those who are
preservers and protectors of 'the wild' and
'the rural' who protest most loudly about
'peace and quiet', reinforcing their bolted
stable doors while incapable of seeing
that the stallions of absurdity and the
daymares are loose and madly coupling.

Under siege, these hard-nosed,
commonsense essentialists have found
that memories of, and nostalgia for, walls
serve just as well as the walls themselves.
When the UK government recently
threatened to 'sell off' its forests, the
conservative uproar was more about an
idea – English woodland – than trees.
The times turn Jill and Joshua Public
into Cathars: worshipping the ideal and
dissing the thing.

Again, no bad thing from my point of
view.

For what the globalisation of the megalo-
polis and the hyper-nostalgia of its
enemies have, synergically, produced
is a phantasmagoria of anachronisms,
dissolutions, dilutions, ironies, absurdities,
accelerations, chimeras, overwritings,
overreachings, blurtings out and miracles
(all generously illustrated in this short
pamphlet). There are ploughman's lunches,
poetry competitions, Harvester eateries,
environmental impact reports, Rhodi-
bashings, rare breeds and alien invasions;
horses are eaten and witchcraft has come
to the attention of the Metropolitan Police.
Kitsch, retro, the procession of sequels,
the exponentially increasing consumption
of drama (London once had two theatres,
now home cinemas are ubiquitous); it may
not be pretty, but everyday life is being
aestheticised and fiction upstaged by
'reality'.

Control and power are practised in the
name of devolution and libertarianism,
interventions are made in the name of
naturalness and spontaneity, and copies are
sold expensively in the name of creativity.
If you visit a castle you will almost
certainly pass through a Visitors Centre
that looks like a motorway service station...
(as I write this, on a train, I look out of
the window and there, on a suburban
running track, piled up at the edge of
the water jump, are six or seven white
steeplechase barriers and on top perches
an immense buzzard) ...everywhere, awash
with tales of disenchantment, pessimism
and homogeneity, loneliness, separateness
and crassness, are the most miraculously
sublime and brazen assemblages,
everywhere is the chance lovemaking of
opposites and attractive unlikes.

Yet mostly we seem to notice very little
of this, and even less to savour it. So
much in the visionary landscape with
its circus of philosophising objects,
floating texts and people-machines goes
unremarked. Esoteric symbols in petrol
station logos, accidental poems made
by the breaking of signposts, bathetic
business names and massive geometrical
puns go ignored. If we really did live
in the 'instant gratification' society of
right wing commentators' imaginations,
then the correction of this sensual deficit
would be a far higher priority than
reducing the burden of government
debt. A short, sharp, shocking
hypersensitisation would be ordered.

Of course, the most crass and
sentimental examples of enchanted
objects pop up as curios on YouTube
for a few hundred thousand hits – the
spook hills, mystery houses and 'knob-
joke' signage – and no harm in that, but
it is a massive missing-of-the-point. Not
because such clips demean (I like de-
meaning) the absurd, but rather that they
de-normalise it, they split it into either
trash or transcendence. They separate
Edgar Allan Poe's 'man' from his 'crowd'.
I, on the other hand, am interested in
what falls between these stinking stools
(yes, it's all excrescence 'in the end', but
for a precious while we choose).

The pleasures to be shared in dreadful,
hilarious juxtapositions (a squirrel
peeping through the eyeholes of a
discarded zombie mask, a sea whipped
into a bubble bath) are available
everywhere; an overwhelming everyday
is infused all over the place with small-
scale tragedies, humble canyons of
vibrant materiality and linguistic farces,
punctuated by brief respites and palate-
cleansing courses of soothing bleakness
and souring concrete symmetries, only
for multi-coloured lichen, punning
signage and accidentally obscene window
displays to abruptly pile richness upon
richness.

Shifting ands

The illustrations in this pamphlet
constitute an alarm, an early warning
system for detecting the approach of
jouissance (the simultaneous enjoyment
of property, including self-dispossession,
of rights and of ecstasy; a feeling so
good it not only hurts but it turns one
thing into everything else); a bobbing
float at the end of your line of senses.
When you see the equivalents of the
illustrations here beginning to twitch
in the optic flow around you, then that
will be a sign to you that the surface of
the landscape is about to give way to the
sinkholes of id. Nonsense follows. Stick
with it; the accidental pun and the chance
obscenity are often brutal doorkeepers
to subtler pleasures in the fabric of the
portal itself.

The pedestrian figures here were all
intended by some designer as generic
representations; yet to the glad eye they
display their eccentricities, amputations,
stretch marks, wrinkles, prostheses and
rearrangements. They serve as a *memento
mutabis* ("remember you will change"),
a reminder of your body as unfinished
business, inscribed into its path and
subject to all that passes along it, a
history made on the hoof.

The signs here are short poems written
after the death of the author. They are
misprints. Letters fall off, palimpsests
wear out to reveal lower and older layers.
The names of giant organisations fade
into brickwork. Meanings float free and
legal entities atomise.

The objects pictured here are vibrant;
their materiality is ready to kick you,
trip you up, glint, roll, tumble and react.
These things transform into props,
displays, commodities, rubbish, junk,
treasures, collectors' items, clues, set
dressing, costumes, insignia, badges,
mascots, evidence, sacraments, signposts,
milestones, markers, totems, fetishes and
lucky charms. Once you become alive
to the vital matter of things you will
realise that these objects are not inert,
but are endlessly wandering up and down
a continuum that includes obsolescence,
sacramentality and commercial exchange.

The places portrayed here seem to have wandered in from somewhere else; looking like discarded architects' models that have swelled in the rain, or what remains of stages when theatres burn down, the spatial equivalents of pregnant pauses and quantum vacuums with the ever-present probability of things just popping into existence and popping straight out again. These are geographical affordances, offers and invitations to step into and interfere.

The School of Management, watch us grow

The simulacra are especially sensitive
to shifts in all things. Copies without
originals, they are always holding out
their hands for something, testing
the waters, begging recognition,
manipulating shadows and golden hours
of sunlight, crying out: "adopt us now!"
and "what's for pudding?" These unstable
and demanding elements were once
characteristic of edgelands, but now
that the edges have sunk deeper into the
tissues of town and country, becoming
essential inserts in their major organs,
the peripheries now pass each other
going in opposite directions; they are
liable to crop up anywhere.

Since the overcoming of things by
their images in the second half of
the twentieth century, simulacra have
assumed, much to their disgust, an iconic
status. This is a painful irony for them!
In search of origins, some genealogy
at least, they have been put to work by
philosophers (Monsieur Baudrillard,
stand up) as symbolic Poe-esque 'men
of the crowd', nameless, inscrutable and
incapable of recognising their Creator
(the Spectacle), insensate to that web
of social relations that has elevated
everything to their own status: orphans
without evidence of a womb, copies
without a creative act.

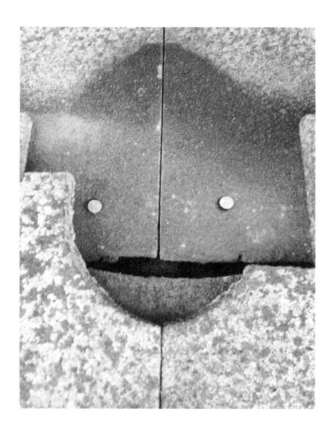

The truth, though, is closer to Poe's,
for these things display contradictory
absences of quality; they are culturally
impoverished in a flashy way, made of
the most vital materials they always have
some blemish through which we glimpse
either animal teeth or stolen jewelry.
They are cool and intense, terrible
fun, and they are ill-disposed to being
anyone's objective correlative. Far from
being the gauleiters of a Baudrillardian
totalitarianism of the unreal, they are the
phantom guides that underwhelm and
so escape it. If we ape their laisser-faire
attitude where selfhood is concerned we
will not go far wrong, but we will go far.

The various absurd elements here –
figures, objects, signs, places, simulacra
– separately or in dynamic relations with
one another, hint at general patterns
of changeableness, mobility, the
ubiquity of irony and the superiority of
accidental symbolism. More importantly,
they serve as recalcitrantly specific
things, placing a restrictive friction
on smooth generalisations, causing a
distorting torque in the smooth spaces
of postmodernism and globalisation.
Once you have accustomed yourself to
identifying these flinty, spiky, enchanted
elements and their trajectories in almost
every space you go, you will begin to
sense how your realisation can be more
than contemplative; how varying your
relation to them can change the pattern
of their own relations with each other.

Rather than simple phantoms of
unreality, these are the real, gothic,
bloody, terrifying thing.

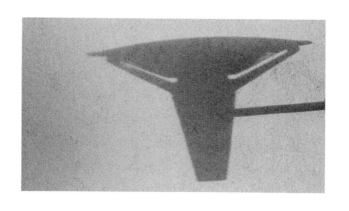

For those not yet tuned to the increasing
frequency of such manifestations of
enchanted matter, help is at hand from
unexpected quarters. The miasma of
cultural residue – those TV shows and
movies that hang about the bus stops and
shop fronts of our memories like surly
teenage phantoms – serves as a fluid
map of a liquid conurbation, a reverse
portal to the vitality of matter; freeing,
liquefacting and animating objects
that once seemed to lack objectives but
now come on like method actors in the
intensity of their motivation.

**CAUTION
Fragile roof**

When transferred from the screens to
the streets, the dramatisation of life
finds its home; space where everything is
engaged in the melodramas of commerce,
erosion, distribution, sedimentation,
condensation and migration; where you
can imagine yourself as the last survivor
of the coming zombie apocalypse, as
a cupid matching strangers, or as a
detective in a neighbourhood where
everyone is suspect. Bathed in the
memory of old TV series, damaged
commodities and discarded wrappers
take on the poignancy of crossroads
tragedies. Things rise and rot, aspire
and fall (celebrated in the vitalism of
anthropologist Jane Bennett and the
object-oriented ontology of philosopher
Graham Harman).

Every rock takes a swing back at anyone
who dares kick it; as Dr Johnson well
knew. Now, such is the velocity of the
circulation of objects and images, that
a huge excess of energy, a free energy
that is surplus to requirements, that is
erotic and creative, is constantly being
generated, spun off and wasted, spilling
across the planet, collecting in gyres
of plastic waste for orgiastic mid-ocean
circle dances; now, the rocks are getting
their retaliation in first.

This super-excess, only good for war,
love, non-procreative sex and spectacle,
the 'accursed share' of irrecuperable
surplus from what Georges Bataille called
the "general (rather than commercial)
economy" magnifes the surpluses created
by the exploitation of cognitive labour
and the massive mental-landgrabs of
companies like Google and Facebook
who make workers of their consumers,
producing wares fashioned from their
own interior and now privatised lives;
and tourism.

The exponential increase in such
productions of unusable intellectual
property and the acceleration of its
circulation are importing an immense
fictional charge to our immediate terrains
and everyday worlds, which, if tapped,
would spring the ordinary apart in a
fabulously catastrophic de-normalisation,
so profound there would be no values
left to speak of; no difference or diversity
would remain, leaving only 'whatever'
and multiplicity to pick over the pieces.
Despite all this, we rarely sense the
beautiful corpse in the next room, or hear
the tick of narrative under the table, or
intuit the invisible in the antique static.

Everywhere, the abject is taught as
litter, transformation as polluting and
transcendence and transfiguration as too
high a security risk; instead of enjoying
such problems, people are encouraged to
believe that there are solutions to them.
Where some niches of gratuitousness
arise to soak up a little of the energy,
they are highly specialised. If social
sexualisation is spreading, then it is
as separated as old cream; confined to
screens and lay-bys at specific times of
the day. Surveys suggest that people
are having less sex in their sexualised
culture. I advocate the dispersal of our
desires to the landscape simply on the
grounds of practicality: they will be
reciprocated there.

The magic stuff, the terrain of enchanted
things, is no relief from the humdrum;
once you hypersensitise yourself to the
full blast of contemporary landscape's
intensity, the banal comes as a blessed
relief from absurdity's ubiquity.
Life is then a thing of challenging
pleasures punctuated by brief periods
of recharging the batteries and
indeterminable periods during which
cruel death slowly emerges as what
determines.

Tentacle thing

And will all this land in our collective lap?

No. It is accessed by the active deployment of senses that reach out into and around the world and its double, that titillate and generously embrace their objects, that squirm like lophophores upon gyrating tentacles, simultaneously going with and manipulating the tides, currents and flows of things to jouissant ends. This work is no virtue; it is what is necessary for perception. Give in to it, let the tentacles unfurl, and the phantasmagoria begins, the million curtains open and the bones begin to dance in the castle of saucepans.

Doing the tentacle-thing is to take
walking a step beyond walking, a
tentative toeing of the possibility that
it might not be enough, that it might be
time to risk an aggressive, futurist and
fascistic return of the body. Doing the
tentacle thing is to embrace the non-
rational in order to make a leap between
mythogeographical walking and some
kind of non-specialist, non-regimented
dance; not the ordered and objectified
choreography of ballet schools and
clubbing, but that dance that has already
rejected most of itself for a way for
human beings to explore in action their
embodied inner selves. So it becomes a
means without an end, a complement
to and a cancelling out of the unusable
surplus, a thinking with the body, a
change of gait from a mythogeographical
to a mythosomatic one.

When walking in relation to the terrain
is complemented by a dancing in relation
to entangled inner and outer lives (what
the choreographer Siriol Joyner calls
"mining", the extractive counterpart to
our construction of an inner landscape),
then this is where the resources of an
otherwise irrecuperable surplus can be
spent: in the reconstruction of interiority.
But the starting point is not within,
subjectivity has been too damaged
recently to sustain a simple quietist
mysticism. Instead, the increasing
scatterings of enchanted objects in the
streets are the required things 'ready-
to-hand' (or rather, escaping Heidegger,
'ready-to-tentacle') to fashion new inner
landscapes of terrain-desire.

We can step out of the flow of
commodities to engage with these
irrecuperable objects, objects which
cannot be exchanged, in economically
redundant spaces; part-objects which are
not wholly produced by our tentacle-
dance but are fulfilled, generalised,
consumed and further enchanted by it.
Let us risk incorporation in a demiurgic-
entrepreneurialism in order to steal its
thunder, to set out 'on the road', nomad
rather than salesperson, to generalise
and distribute the refrains of the tentacle
dance!

You will soon see your doppelganger
jiving with its real double.

"It's shifting, Hank!"

Of course, there is a downside to all this making manifest of absurd, ironic and accidental art; while in hyper-finance it no longer applies, in soul accountancy a credit somewhere is a debit somewhere else. The emergence, from the shadows, of so many enchanted things is part of an even more general impoverishment of our inner lives, a dragging out into the light of things that need darkness. Hence the efficacy of redeploying these surplus excretions in the making of entangled interior and exterior landscapes during some kind of heightened physical immersion and engagement of thinking with the body.

But will some kind of dance –
choreographies that anyone can dance
anywhere – be sufficiently well paced to
take advantage of this condition? Mobile
and yet sufficiently pedestrian to allow
the senses to entangle with material and
textual wonders?

Each step, each figure, gesture and spell
– in whatever form, walk or dance –
now becomes a potential first towards a
new corporeal and aesthetic nomadism,
putting a torque upon the dominant
hypermobility of things and images;
distorting, defamiliarising and re-making
them while still in motion. The architect-
walker is the body awaited by the
sedentary majority, coming to rearrange
the future (long in the planning) from
the ruins of the past, both its broken
structures and broken dreams, jumbling
time so as to dance as superhuman,
posthuman and human simultaneously.
To walk with things. To shapeshift – and
then to, simply, shift.

The curling and writhing, swinging and
gyrating, grabbing and interpreting
narratives and their unbounded doubles,
dug or dispersed, describe the meshwork
that has replaced the cities and the fields
and the wilds beyond. These rambling
stories, weaving pathetic fallacies and
human choices in exemplary narratives,
signal a world far closer to the nomadic
than it has been for some time, a world
that may be subjected to massive
migrations of climate refugees, and
shiftings of labour as natural resources
fail and laboratories and lecture halls
are drowned, as the distinctions between
tourism, work, sectarianism and
economics increasingly liquefy.

The nomads of the past were hybrids:
human/horse/bow-and-arrow. They were
highly cultured, but hugely violent. In
order to protect their temporary 'turf'
they needed to be. It is the same today,
on a far smaller scale: "we do fighting
well" a young woman from a showman's
(fairground owning) family told me the
other day. But maybe the nomadic hybrids
can be different this time: a combination
of dancer-extended-organism/virtuality/
stranger-ethics? Rearranging worlds in
which we all shift about in material and
non-material meshworks of family and
friendship, assembling and reassembling
communities/choreographies, de-
territorialising and re-territorialising, in
which roots become rhizomes (just as the
frozen 'old ones' of Mynyddoedd Y Preseli
became the bluestones of Stonehenge).

We will take our roots with us like the
Walking Palm (*Socratea exorrhiza*) of
the rainforests, pre-empting our arrivals,
always already elsewhere, entangling our
departures virtually with our destinations,
moving first digitally and then physically;
emoting and grasping at the future with
digital tentacles, their toothy pads hooked
on, besotted by and infatuated with new
entanglements. Anti-nostalgic, puncturing
the crusts of identity and racial nonsense
by stranger ethics; by the assumption
that, good or bad, the stranger is holy and
always to be offered hospitality, a partner
to be improvised with; which is understood
all the more when we make ourselves
strangers, practising strangerhood.

This will be to realise the proverb of
St Victor of Hugo that I have quoted,
uniquely, in both *Mythogeography* and *On
Walking*:

"Only the person for whom the whole
world is like a foreign country is perfect."

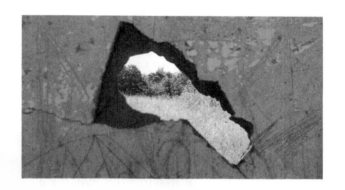

Little of this happens without new synaptic
flesh, an exploring and unfinished
body and an ambulatory nomadic
mind that entangles with signs, things,
simulacra, figures, virtual prostheses...
and with strangers. It continues with a
new kind of journey, an experimental
pilgrimage without destinations, a
mental-physical nomadism in which we
can place ourselves 'at the mercy' of the
road, moving symbolically and schizo-
cartographically, preparing the way for a
chosen mass wandering, choreographing
ourselves, pre-empting and trumping the
ends of the earth by getting there before
it gets to us.

By meeting the terminal world halfway,
implementing Zeno's paradox and
endlessly delaying ends in ambiguous
shrines, we ensure that we are always a
slightly shorter half way to apocalypse
every day.

About the Author

Phil Smith has written over 100 works
for theatre and created many site-specific
theatre projects, often with Exeter-based
Wrights & Sites [www.mis-guide.com].

He is Associate Professor at Plymouth
University and has published papers
in *Studies In Theatre and Performance,
Cultural Geographies, Performance Research*
and *New Theatre Quarterly,* co-authored a
range of *Mis-Guides* and written or co-
written several other books including:
*On Walking …and Stalking Sebald,
Mythogeography, Counter-Tourism: The
Handbook* and *A Pocketbook, A Sardine
Street Box of Tricks.*

Explore further at:
www.triarchypress.net/smithereens